Today, I will...

Daily Challenges for Getting and Staying Out of That Rut

D. A. MICHAELS

We all need to be encouraged or challenged, sometimes every day, to make better choices in our lives—to set some goals. This book is filled with thoughts to help motivate you come up with your own ideas, setting your own "today's" goals for tomorrow's success and growth. Enhance your character, build your self-esteem, become a better person, and, mostly, love your life better.

D. A. MICHAELS

Today I will...
be kind,
especially
to those
who aren't
kind to me.

Today, I will...

face one of my fears.

Today, I will...

choose
to forgive.

Today

I will...

remain calm.

Today, I will…

make
time to
relax.

Today, I will…

face my past.

the possible criminal connection of the heavy men ... eventually taken away. These people knew everyth... everyone and were not slow in discussing it. There was n... reserve, self-preservation.

Rosemary had talked about it being natural that peop... assume she was gay since she was single and had a sister w... already 'out' with a partner who was a lawyer. Gertie had s... about her husband's problems coping with drink and violen... spoke as if Jack had been prone to getting chest colds in the w... Colm had approached their table with a casual apology ov... incident as if it had not been the most excruciatingly embarra... moment of her life. The two women had told her how they ... initially thought Ria was mad to go to America and leave ... children but they hoped it would all work out for the best.

Marilyn could not take in the degree of involvement and inde... interference that these people felt confident to have in everyon... else's life. They thought nothing of discussing the motives an... private sorrows of their friend with Marilyn who was after all a ... complete stranger, here purely because of an accidental home ... exchange. While she felt sympathy for Ria and all that had ... happened to her, she also felt a sense of annoyance.

Why had she not kept her dignity, and refused to allow all these ... people into her life? The only way to cope with tragedy and grief ... was to refuse to permit it to be articulated and acknowledged. Deny ... its existence and you had some hope of survival. Marilyn got out of ... bed and looked down on the messy garden and the other large red ... brick houses of the neighbourhood. She felt very lost and alone in ... this place where garrulous people wanted to know everything about ... you and expected you to need the details of their lives too!

She ached for the cool house and beautiful garden in Westville. If ... she were there now she could go and swim lengths of her pool safe ... in the knowledge that no one would call and burden her with post ... mortems about last night. Clement the cat who slept on her bed ... every night woke up and stretched and came over to her hopefully. ... He was purring loudly. The day was about to begin, he was ... expecting a game and a bowl of something.

Marilyn looked at him sadly. 'I don't usually talk to animals, ... Clement, but I'm making an exception in your case. I made the ... wrong decision coming here. It was the worst decision I ever made ... in my life.'

CHAPTER SIX

'Do you think when we're talking to Granny we should call her Nora?' Brian asked.

'What?' Annie looked up from her book.

'You know ... if we call Bernadette's mother by her first name maybe we should do the same with Granny.' Brian wanted to be fair.

'No, Brian, and shut up,' said Annie.

'You always say shut up, you never say anything nice, not ever at all.'

'Who could say anything nice to you, Brian, honestly?'

'Well, some people do.'

'Who apart from Mam and Dad? And they *have* to because you're what they got.'

'Finola often says nice things.'

'Tell me one nice thing she said to you today, go on tell me.'

'She said it was good that I had remembered to let my knights command the centre of the board.'

'And had you?' Annie still refused chess lessons and she couldn't accept that Brian had mastered it.

'Well, only by accident in a way. I just sort of put them out there and they were commanding and she was very pleased with me.' Brian smiled at the triumph of it all.

Sometimes he was more pathetic than awful, Annie thought, you'd feel sorry for him. And he didn't really understand that their lives were going to change. He thought that after the summer

Today, I will…

turn off
my phone
and read
a book.

Today, I will...
drink water.
Only.

Today, I will…

eat a meal
sitting down
before leaving
for work.

Today

I will...

speak an
encouraging word
to someone.

Today, I will…

write
something
in my journal.

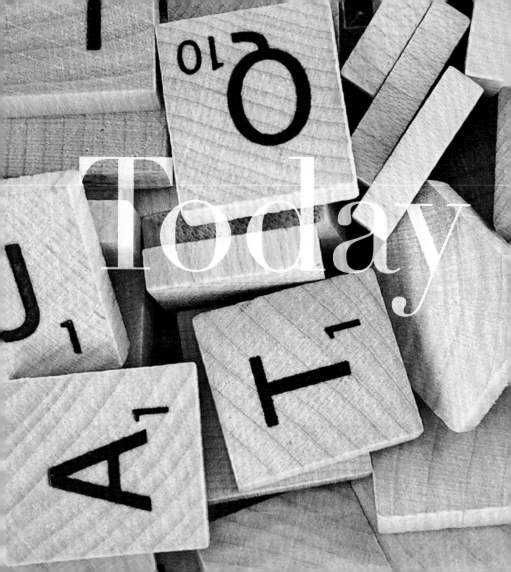

I will...

learn one
new word.

Today, I will…
get eight
hours
of sleep.

Today, I will

take the stairs, not the elevator.

Today

I will...

go for a walk.

Today, I will...
re-evaluate
my priorities.

LIVE **FULLY**
CREATE **HAPPINE**
SPEAK **KINDLY**
HUG **DAILY**
SMILE **OFTEN**
HOPE **MORE**
LAUGH **FREELY**
SEEK **TRUTH**
INSPIRE **CHANGE**
LOVE **DEEPLY**

Today

I will...

wake up
thirty minutes
earlier
for personal
meditation.

Today

I will...

make time
for exercise.

Today
I will...

not use any vulgar words.

Today, I will... not buy anything.

Today

I will...

not say
one word
of complaint.

Today, I will…

eat nothing containing processed sugar.

Today

I will...

use cash only.

Today, I will…
not turn on
the televsion.
Period.

Today

I will...

not eat
anything
unhealthy
between
meals.

Today, I will. . .

not gossip.

Today I will...

not drink
any coffee.

Today, I will…

make my bed before leaving the room.

Today

I will...

only ask God
for guidance.

Today, I will...

say
"thank you"
at least once.

Today I will

write a letter
to an old friend.

Today, I Will...

© 2018 KPT Publishing, LLC
Written by D. A. Michaels

Published by KPT Publishing
Minneapolis, Minnesota 55406
www.KPTPublishing.com

ISBN 978-1-944833-51-0

Designed by AbelerDesign.com

First printing December 2018

10 9 8 7 6 5 4 3 2 1

Printed in the United States of America